CW01665527

IT'S OK
IT'S OK
IT'S OK
IT'S OK
IT'S OK
IT'S OK
IT'S OK
IT'S OK
IT'S OK
IT'S OK
IT'S NOT OK.

LOCKDOWN: STORIES FROM A SHADOW PANDEMIC

Writing on the Wall
Toxteth Library
Windsor Street, Liverpool
L8 1XF

Published by Writing on the Wall, 2021

This edition published in 2023

Edited by: Liverpool Publishing Agency

Design and layout by Katrina Paterson

ISBN: 978-1-910580-51-6

0151 703 0020
info@writingonthewall.org.uk
www.writingonthewall.org.uk

Stay up to date with our latest books, projects, courses, and events with our newsletter. Sign up on our website www.writingonthewall.org.uk

WRITING ON THE WALL

Contents

Introduction

Why is this book important?

I've been trying to put together the introduction for this book for quite some time. I was struggling to find the words to describe the devastating impact domestic abuse has and to firmly contextualise it in todays' society. What I do know concretely is that this book is very important.

Domestic abuse will affect 1 in 4 women in their lifetimes. An alarming but tired statistic. One we've all heard before, so, I think it's important here to look at domestic abuse prior to the Covid-19 pandemic. The Office for National Statistics reported that 80 women were killed by a current or ex-partner between April 2018 and March 2019 – **a 27 per cent increase on the year before.** Do I need to say these are only the convicted cases, the cases filed murder instead of manslaughter, the cases that were reported, where a body was found? These are the 'extreme' cases, the one offs, the physical abuse displayed instead of the emotional, mental and financial. 100 calls are made to the police on average every hour regarding domestic abuse. Another alarming statistic. In 2017 it was reported that there had been a 25% cut to funding for domestic abuse services since 2010. One year later, research found that one in ten refuges and one in five community-based services received no local authority funding, a figure that has surely risen in the past few years. Things were already pretty bad.

Then came Covid19.

Many of us sat alone, forced inside with the real threat to our physical health outside our very windows. But what was inside the confines of our homes could potentially be much, much worse for some of us. The statistics were more than frightening, they highlighted a potential collapse of the services that were set up to protect victims in the first place. The government not only failed to provide increased emergency intervention services but completely ignored the need to support survivors who were further along their journey to recovery. Survivors who may be forced back to a partner or who's progress may deteriorate when trapped inside without support. For a long time there feels there has been little action taken to tackle domestic abuse at the root too. Looking at how we view relationships and gender roles, how we communicate, to how we parent would mean reforming and restructuring patriarchal systems in a time when some of us genuinely believe we have reached gender equality. A place were so many of us perpetuate the idea we're 'doing it for ourselves' yet are still too frightened to publicly discuss abuse for fear of being shamed or misunderstood. A society were only 18% of us are reporting our abuse to the police.

According to the website Research in Practice[1] during the pandemic 'there was a 25% increase in calls to Refuge's domestic abuse helpline, with visits to the helpline website showing 150% increase. Similarly, Women's Aid have reported a 41% increase in the organisation's live chat service since the lockdown began.' Despite these horrifying figures the government announced new plans to allocate a mere £22 million to 548 community organisations, working out at around £40,000 on average per organisation. Considering the cuts to funding in the first place and a huge increase in need, this simply isn't enough.

And so back to the question – why is this book important? As a nation we are in danger of becoming desensitised to domestic abuse and gender-based violence. It happens behind closed doors, in often what we determine to be 'safe' places. And when we do see stories play out in public these incidents are usually relayed to us as something that happened to the victim, leaving the perpetrator completely out of the narrative. The simple statement, 'they were abused', removes the perpetrator entirely, moving responsibility away from them and onto the victim. That's the power of language.

But it connects us too.

This book is full of words. It's full of stories, of life, of laughter, of survival, pain, determination and

1 (https://www.researchinpractice.org.uk/all/news-views/2020/april/domestic-abuse-in-the-coronavirus-epidemic/

everything in between. These stories are communicating with us. They demand we recognise the real human experience within abuse and not just the stats. It forces us to see the experiences of our sisters, mothers, fathers, daughters, neighbours. It's a call to arms, an unapologetic account of modern-day 'love'.

It's Not Ok was a 12-week creative writing course that worked alongside women who have experience of domestic abuse. The project was part of our What's Your Story? (WYS) programme that employs a groupwork methodology to help communities come together, share, write and publish their work. We have been delivering projects like this for over a decade and our new online writing centre The Writer's Bloc has allowed us to deliver three new WYS projects, It's Not Ok, Time to Breathe and Write Minds. Our group met online weekly for writing sessions led by scriptwriter and teacher Margy McShane.

I have been in my job for nearly five years now. I have worked on at least twenty WYS projects, each always critically important and deeply moving. These projects are the coming together of individuals with shared life experience and often trauma. It's the uncovering of new creative tools that helps us express ourselves, communicate our histories and, perhaps most importantly, our hopes. But really, the key to all of this is the group; the magic lies in the sharing and listening. Finding common ground, celebrating difference and reaching out to support someone, means the group moves forward together.

Within two weeks it was obvious what a special group we were working with and how vitally important it was in this moment of enforced stillness. Some of us had brand new realisations, often like a freight train screaming past in the middle of the night. Some of us were forced to confront our fear of being alone, maybe we learnt to trust ourselves a little more, practice self-care (which isn't always pretty), but our common ground was what we were all feeling - sometimes so intensely we couldn't make sense of it.

And how the writing improved. As we felt, we wrote. We made sense of ourselves, our worlds and we found our voices again. When we didn't commit to the writing for a week, we knew, and we helped each other. Writing is hard but turning up can be hard too. And we did hard things together.

I would like to thank the WoW team who worked tirelessly throughout the pandemic to support our communities and provide creative opportunities like these. To The Liverpool Editing Company for their dedication and commitment, to all the agencies across Merseyside who referred participants onto the course and who never receive the praise they so deserve. Thank you to writer and course leader Margy McShane, who never faltered, without your dedication this book would not be possible. But to the group I'd like to say the biggest congratulations. Some of you might not see how courageous you are just yet, but your words in this book speak for themselves. Keep writing.

And for our readers, a simple request. Share this book with as many people as you can. If you can hear us, then you can see and maybe then we can start to bring about change together.

Emma Hulme
WoW Programme Manager

What's Your Story?
It's Not OK

Earn My Love

Cheryl Cain

To whom it may concern
You really ought to know
I won't hand it on a plate
This will be a bumpy road

I won't try to understand you
I won't heal your broken heart
I won't tell you all my secrets
Or share my broken parts

I won't let you make me feel bad
I won't let you take control
I won't let you isolate me
You won't make me feel alone

I will never change to please you
I won't worry if we clash
I will stand true to my boundaries
To the ground they'll never crash

I won't invest early on
My empathy will be on ice
My judgement will be reserved
It never pays to be *too* nice

As we chat I will observe you

Be aware of every move
Look out for red flags flying
Reject you if I choose

I demand that you are worthy
I insist that you are whole
I must know that you respect my freedom
My passions, my loves, my goals

I won't offer you an apology
It's just the way it is
I made a pinkie promise to me
I sealed it with a kiss

Bee in a Biscuit Tin

Cheryl Cain

In the dying light of summer
A bee, dead, curled
As a child in its last slumber
Is solemnly prepared for burial

Two girls, flaxen hair, wisps
Blowing as autumn breathes its first chilly breaths
Work solemnly to prepare the fallen aviator
For his final flight

He is laid lovingly in a biscuit tin
Cushioned by the delicate, wasted petals
Of his short life
The tissue paper blooms, sickly sweet
So industriously tended

In hushed, respectful whispers they work
Intent, focused, as one
Creating, moulding, a soft, dark, earthy haven
Where he can rest

In the summer worn garden
As pansies ruffle in the September breeze
Their ritual complete
The girls stand, heads bowed, a last farewell
To their summer friend

The sleepy buzz of sunny days

United in tribute they turn
Laughing, skipping, swinging high
Feet flying
Skimming the washing line
Dancing in metallic skies

In My Victorian Tin

Cheryl Cain

There's a Victorian tin, I keep my memories in
I stow away a sliding, slithering secret
Coiled in a corner, its heart still beating
I lock in jeering, ugly laughter of teenage boys
Sharp like gravel embedded in a knee
I tenderly wrap in tissue fluttering girlhood dreams
Raped by ignorant gargoyles

There's a Victorian tin, I keep my memories in
I force into the depths sharp, slicing slander
Juvenile harpies, eyes blue rimmed, lip gloss suffocating
I swipe away a wicked, wizened whisper sending it crashing
A ravaged rainbow roars for revenge
I suffocate the spectre of a rotting friendship
Languishing like a collapsing corpse

There's a Victorian tin, I keep my memories in
I fold away love letters which gibber and gabble
Driven mad with false hopes and poisoned pen promises
I slap the twisted face of a scornful village
Defiling and desiccating the air with its violent breath
I swaddle with sorrow the feared child, innocent
Cut away like a tormented tumour from my soul

My Victorian tin weighs cold and heavy
Youth and beauty fading, echoing shadows of past
Whispers of what might have been
Regrets stinging like hailstone

As softly whispering corn sings its mournful lullaby
I kiss goodbye to the cherished child in my mind's eye
Allow the glow of my son's smile to warm my frozen parts
Hold hands with the shy girl in the pollen-stained dress

One Day I Knew

Cheryl Cain

One day I knew
It was not OK
In a cosy room, safe, removed
Like a passenger on a high-speed train
Catching glimpses of a life endured
Flinching flashes through safety glass
The bang, slam of a door
The smash, clash of metal on glass
A frightened fluttering heart
Like a captured bird cradled
Close to my breast

One day I knew
I was not alone
Surrounded by warrior women
Proud Amazonian homemakers
Separate yet silently bonded
Dignified mother soldiers tending wounds
I drew strength in No Man's Land

One day I knew
We were worth more
Bloody from treading on eggshell shards
Stealthy double-agent, plotting
Masquerading under frozen smiles
Enduring poison ivy touches

Parrying probing search lights of paranoia
Wearing welts from barbed wire words
Shielding you from roaring, ragged anger
Navigating minefields of treachery and hurt
I packed our lives into a white van of hope

One day I knew
The worst was behind us
On familiar fields, birds released
Dancing in sun-soaked skies
Soaring high, harmonious
Battle scars healing, whole
Wearing single-mumdom proudly
Like vibrant, shimmering plumage
Stretching kaleidoscope wings
Teaching you to fly high

Planes of Freedom

Cheryl Cain

Breathe in cool fresh air
Spread strong arms, muscles flexing
Wind soft on proud face

Craft a warm, safe den
Boundaries forged from iron
Impenetrable

Create my own rules
Break them, no retribution
Change them, as I grow

Explore new landscapes
Bright colours, fresh faces
Standing out in herds

Roar with confidence
Reclaim my crown, Lioness
Protector of Hope

Nurture Family
Gather community
Walk tall, lead my pack

Worthy warrior
Demanding real love, joyful sex

Indomitable

Strengthen my body
Raise head on elegant neck
Poised for action

Feed my starving mind
With words, rhyme, rhythm;
Fuel feminist fire

Shed binding shackles
Empowering lost sisters
Fire, trailing bright

Up high surveying
My kingdom, planes of freedom
Ready to claim life

Something Terrible

Cheryl Cain

'Something terrible happened last night.' The boy looked up with wide, chocolate-brown eyes. 'But I'm not allowed to talk about it.'

She was struck by the grave eyes and solemn mouth, on this child's ruddy, soft-cheeked face. Such a heart-achingly beautiful boy, all-knowing and sad. Those intent eyes openly inviting questions for a fleeting second and then – the moment was gone. She could almost hear the cold grating shutters slamming down. His face rigid and unyielding.

'Can I help?'

Straddling his battered bike he fiddled with his sleeve in studied concentration.

'Nah, Mum says it's done now. Nothing anyone can do.'

He mimicked his brash mother's exact intonation, his words leaden with the finality of it all.

'Gotta go. She'll go mad if I'm late for tea.'

She watched him pedal away, track-suited legs pumping like chubby pistons, the weight of his untold secret sitting heavy on his handlebars.

Modern Day Fairytale

Cheryl Cain

Why does he frown so much, deep etched lines grooved into his forehead, eyes cold like the steel of a huntsman's knife?
Why does he show his angry face even when the sun spreads its fingers, tickling our eyelids through early morning blinds, beckoning us out to feel the gentle whispering breeze wash over our faces?
Why does his dark brooding shadow block out the light, chilling the air like a hulking ogre dwarfing out the regal sun?
Why does his disapproving, closed face make the air thick with tension, smothering our faces like a conjured mask?
Why do we speak in hushed tones like we do at the library with its comforting book smell and dusty adventures on shelves?
Why do you make me place things down so carefully as if they were as fragile as a delicate painted dragon egg, careful not to make a sound and attract his all-seeing gaze?
Why do you tiptoe past him at a safe distance as if he were a snarling, blood-thirsty monster from a dark fairytale best left to slumber?
Why does he keep the house so quiet and empty like a lonely enchanted castle on a windswept hill, guarding it against the intruders that never come?

Why does he sneer at your beautiful princess voice and pretty smile, your warm snuggly hugs and soft loving touch?
Why does he make you jump like a jittering, wild unicorn, shouting and abusing your gentleness with ugly violent words?
Why does he slam and bang and crash his anger into our harmonious togetherness, our world of dress-up games, fairy tales and treasure hunts?
Why does he build a windowless tower of grumpiness and shoutiness around us, hiding the key so we cannot escape?
Why do our laughing, smiling faces make him black inside so that his mouth curls cruelly and his hands lash out like a vengeful beast?
Why does his cursed love make him see poisoned apples in your eyes and dark intent in your heart?
Why does every day he grips tighter, looms larger, sheds his sheep's clothing, you grow straighter and grip strongly your sword?
Why does he howl in pain as you slash our way through thorny walls, scramble through deep, dark woods into the glittering light?
Why does he chase us on a dark, pounding stallion, hunting us, tracking us in the stealthy, ink black night?
Why is he tapping at the window, still waiting patiently outside the door, waiting to steal your heart?

You Came
Cheryl Cain

I remember that child silently screaming, kicking, pounding
Behind a sound-proof glass wall
Restrained, contained by the swamping despair
The head-banging, ear-splitting frustration
As they played
Indifferent, unfettered in the warm summer sun
Spikey, stabbing pain like the rose thorns in our garden

I remember that gentle, muted, wide-eyed child
Walking shyly, uncertainly towards that sly, jagged girl
Snatching, clawing, luring
Away, she grabbed the child's only treasure
That floppy, silly, seventies psychedelic teddy
Defiling, reviling, wiling away
Its unconditional friendship and comfort
Denying her its void filling, love giving presence

I remember, you were suddenly there, like a flare
In the night, a sun burst through the rain
Giggling, skipping, teasing, grinning
Hands entwined, blond heads close, inclined
Moving as one
Conspiring, collecting, creating

Magical worlds, untold adventures, glittering treasures
Playing, swaying, disobeying
Our neat, orderly mother with stern face
Together, in unity, confidants, combatants
Friends forever – Sisters!

Leaving

Cheryl Cain

She looked around. Boxes stood scattered in the cold, naked room, stripped of its identity, the trappings of her life carefully placed into a soft cocoon of bubble wrap. Dust gently fluttered on the floor, newly exposed, its hiding places rudely removed and packed away in the van outside. She could hear the echoes of joyful children playing in the street, unencumbered by adult strife, innocent of life's ruthless labyrinth of twists and turns awaiting them. Upstairs, she could hear the muffled voices of her brother and dad struggling to manoeuvre a bulky bookcase which was proving to be an awkward customer. They argued good-naturedly about how to tackle the stairs. She touched the smooth textured wood of the dining table, caught the faint sweet aroma of beeswax. She remembered choosing the furniture she would leave behind, her chest bursting with happiness, proud that she had finally achieved her ideal of 'family', an oak six-seater dining table with matching dresser. It looked woefully bereft now of its brightly spotted wipe-down tablecloth and Jake's Batman place mat.

In the faint distance she heard the melodic chimes of a church clock somewhere. She looked at her watch. 2pm. She'd have to hurry; he would be back soon. She looked at the growing number of objects she had put to one side. They were an eclectic bunch of oddities. Each one had caused her to pause, as a long-buried memory burst forth unbidden. There was a picture of her and Andy, young and fresh faced, smiling openly into the camera, both clutching a Bud in one hand, arms around waists with the other. She could still smell a mixture of beer and aftershave as she remembered holding onto him, feeling his warm, hard body pressed against hers, lights flashing, boisterous voices raised over the pulsing music. That had been a good night, one of the few. It was back when she thought they would be good together, before she got pregnant. She couldn't even say he'd changed. The signs had all been there. She'd simply ignored them, explained them away. Reasoned with her whining, cajoling inner voice that there were good explanations for his nitrogen ice aloofness, his snarling, crashing temper tantrums, his black, disdainful attitude towards her that over time seemed to fester and spread like a stinking, putrid wound.

A glittering trinket caught her eye. She examined the tacky silver bracelet, brittle, clasps sharp, scratching against her skin. It had been an apology gift after one of Andy's meltdowns. That time he'd smashed the bathroom door with his fist. The crash of raging skin and sinew against splintering wood had sent poor Jake into terrified hysterics. Andy had presented it to her with a flourish as if it could magically rewind time; erase the memory of Jake's wide frightened eyes. She tossed it clattering into the charity box along with the framed photo and then scooped the remaining items into its dark, gaping recesses where they belonged. She had no desire to revisit any more painful reminiscences.

She took a deep breath, scanned the room one last time, taking in the walls marked with the scars of their unhappy life. It was time to go. Her brother and dad were now huffing and puffing through the living room, cheeks red and sweat smeared, with the final offending bookcase tamed into submission. The room shifted and she gripped the back of a chair to steady herself, her legs leaden at the thought of the inevitable confrontation when Andy arrived home to find them gone. She gasped a ragged breath, attempting to stem the rising tide of fear. She'd cross that bridge later. Now it was time to open herself like a fragile butterfly to the possibility of a new chapter, a new start. She felt the warmth of certainty and courage pulsing through her veins warming her numb, cold hands, calming her fluttering heart. She and Jake would be happy; she would make sure of it.

As the last of the boxes were shoved snugly into the white van she turned and looked one last time at the house that had held her captive. It stared back with blank, unseeing eyes. Exhaling deeply, she turned and squeezed into the van next to her brother. 'Ready, Kidda?' She nodded, allowing herself a tentative smile as sandbags of shame and guilt slid into the footwell. A delicate bubble of anticipation began to grow in her chest as they drove away, shiny and new. Ahead of her the tantalizing allure of the unknown beckoned like the sweet smell of a bright new morning after a summer's storm.

The Harbinger

Cheryl Cain

The man stood by the grave. Tall, erect in ill-fitting funeral garb. Slightly separate from the grieving in prime position to observe, soak up every detail of their loss.

The slimy coldness of decaying leaves and damp, mossy stone crawled across the congregation in the icy wind. His cold eyes stared, boring into the scene unfolding before him. The young, anguished wife, pale and drawn, sobbed, holding her son and daughter in comfort perhaps? Or simply to stop her from crumpling down to the floor like a dry, wasted shell spent from all the shocked tears she had cried. Hypnotised by the gentle, monotone drone of the vicar, the children looked blank, numb; mini androids moving sluggishly in their own private nightmare, eyes wide and disbelieving.

He drank in their sorrow, feeling elated, excited, alive. Every detail was received as if in high-definition. He battled with his face to keep the smile that threatened to betray him masked in dignified sympathy. He speculated whether the buffet would be as superior as last week's with those melt-in-the-mouth pastries. He looked at the young woman's scuffed shoes. Probably not.

His thoughts drifted to his mother who would be waiting impatiently for his recount of the day, heaving the weight of her bulk as she craned her neck to see the last of the funeral cars leave. He strode quickly to catch up with the huddled group, cold drizzle tickled his fevered skin, beading on his jacket. As he reached them, the young wife turned, their eyes locking. 'I'm sorry for your loss.' Words in monotone, leaning uncomfortably close, stale breath acrid in her nostrils, the young woman stared, eyes held unwillingly by his direct, searching strobes. A flash of confusion and uncertainty flitting across her face as she sensed this man's longing to connect with her, touch with long, pale fingers the grave-shaped grief which threatened to suck her down into its depths. A wave of revulsion hit her with so much force that she felt the bile scorching her throat. Muttering thank you she turned away, pulling her children to her to shield them from the relentless hollow stare of this spectral man. He stood taking in deep breaths, lungfuls of damp November air; his heart beating erratically in his chest. He felt energized, exhilarated, high on the heady fumes of pain and anguish.

He became aware of one of the group, an elderly lady with bright eyes and a crocheted hat observing him, and quickly smoothed down his mask of propriety. Perhaps it would be best to avoid the wake. It was a sacrifice. He brushed away the rivulets of rain in sharp, jagged motions, irritation making his teeth grind at being cheated of this prime opportunity to drink up the heady scent of funeral flowers, pastries and cloying grief. The elderly woman turned again twittering urgently to her companion. Disquiet ruffled his carefully slicked back, oily hair. She'd be disappointed, anger making her face motionless and stony like a church gargoyle but no, it was time to go. He had outstayed his welcome.

Childhood

Angela Cheveau

Does anyone escape unscathed
from this place?
Patchwork memories stitched
with tears and splashed sunlight
packing our hurt
into suitcases of pain
we carry each other
wherever we go
Mingled histories etched
in our bones
our stories embedded
within us
in circles, patterns, rings of a tree
I remember
star soaked nights
you, Dad
when you carried me
wrapped in blankets
of whisky tinged kisses
her amber light forever
beckoning you
down shadow filled alleyways
where I could not follow
Nights squatting
in pooled shadows
on the stairs, hugging my knees

while voices below split open the sky
The moon looked away
Didn't care
Days, when I smeared words
like war paint
on my face
my book a shield to hide behind
the carpet gaping wide
vast no man's land stretching
between two warring armies
And me
In the middle
soaked in their anger
picking sharp shards of shrapnel
from my bones.
Seeping sadness I spilled over
wetting bed covers
climbing inside books for cover
I wrapped myself in cloaks of words
draped silver strands of stories
round my neck
my mouth spilled sunlight
I wore starlight in my hair
parched paper yellowed with time
crinkled beneath my fingertips
pressed petal pages ached
with the memory of the sun
I drew threads of magic
around my shoulders

too small yet to carry
the weight of these wolves
waiting silently in the shadows
I wandered through forests
bathed in moonlight
the whispering wind softly soothing
searching in circles
for my lost self
Folding up
I made myself small
like Alice
to sit at your mad tea party
With the silence of snowfall
I broke apart slowly
gently
crumbling like a coastal shelf
Later
I would try to trace the pattern
of you in cold marble lips
that spat cut glass kisses
I looked for you
in empty men I could never fill
shut away in the shadows
of bone cold vaults
my voice lost to the winds of time
Now
I pick up my pen and dip it in pain
spattering the blank page with words
spill light into my wounds

peeling myself open, layer by layer
bleeding my story to the weeping sky

Freedom

Angela Cheveau

I want to escape this prison
of sun-splashed bricks and slate
The wings of my soul flutter gently inside my ribs,
aching to break free
this cage of bone
To soar free
unfettered
lifted on the limitless air
I want to feel
I want to feel the gentle ache of a blossom heavy bough
unfurling itself to the watching sky with a blush
I want to feel the whip of the wild wind
conducting an ecstatic symphony through my body,
writing me upon the air
I want to sit in a colour splashed meadow of wildflowers
daintily dancing with the playful breeze
watch butterflies flirting with flowers
I want to watch daisies giggling at the sun
Listen to
sweet syllables of birdsong trickling
the cascading leaves arching above my head
I want to lie on a carpet of grass breathlessly
Watching as dandelion seed ballerinas twirl through the air, whirling

with a soft grace towards
their final, silent bow
I want to lie in a forest glade and become still
I want to listen and breathe in rhythm
with the peaceful cadence of the forest heartbeat
cathedrals of leaves arching above
in quiet devotion to the sky
I want to listen to the whispers of ancient trees
watch as their leaves dapple golden light
tracing delicate patterns upon the hallowed ground.
I want to listen as bluebells offer up
their quiet poetry to the sky
in whispers of lilac
I want to feel the swell of the ocean
cradled in its swaying lullaby
I want to watch as moonlight
paints her fragile silver light across the night
dripping down rooftops, pooling in lamplight
A star-sprinkled sky glittering above
a sequin scarf softly drawn across
the elegant neck of night
I want to feel the swoop of the seagull
gliding through the sun-soaked evening sky
wings tipped with golden light
I want to hear the heavy flap of its wings breaking
the soft hush of the dying day
I want to wrap myself in the melting colours
of the amaranthine sky
the sun turning her back on the day

tossing handfuls of stars over her golden shoulder
I want to feel
I want to be drenched
in crystal showers of rain-washed clarity
I want to hold the diamond glint of a dewdrop
lit by sunlight
fracturing pieces of sky
I want to watch the delicate colours of a rainbow
fade softly like a memory
I want to watch birds fling
hopefully at the sky
handfuls of confetti
I want to toss my soul into the air
let it break free
on the whispering wind
scattering leaves

HIM

Angela Cheveau

Splitting me open
you tore a hole in my soul
through it the light shines

Darkness inside you
attracted my gentle light
a moth to a flame

Battered boundaries
paper thin I watch them tear
like an open wound

You force your way in
a burglar breaking the locks
I am defenceless

Dragged by my ankles
flipped like a prime piece of meat
peppered with poison

Scissor legs spread wide
I lay flat like a pattern
a dress made of skin

Glass kisses that sting

with the sharp edges of spite
from cold marble lips

Mouthfuls of carpet
facedown I drink the stairs dry
to quench your parched soul

A monster crawled out
from under my bed and climbed
inside of my head

Memories seeping
like blood from an open wound
refusing to heal

Broken girl, you are
a warrior, pick up your
shining sword of light

My pen is my sword
transforming dark into light
I will write you out

Dripping in bright light
she stepped out of the darkness
never looking back

The Magic Box
Angela Cheveau

Inside my secret box of magic, I will
Sip the colours of sunset from a cup filled with sky
Wrap ribbons of rainbows round curls of cloud
Toss confetti birds in handfuls across the church of the sky
Trace the paper moon, crinkling its face with charcoal stained fingers
Sizzle slices of buttered sunlight and dip them in an egg yolk sky

Inside my box of magic I will put
Knitted threads of autumn and sew silken strands of burnished gold into a jumper to soak my bones in
Silver dipped seagulls swirling circles of script across pages of paper sky
Crisscrossed shadow nets catching silver-tipped moon fish
The soft suck of succulent spring at the teat of withered winters thawing
Puddles of pooled moonlight spilling silver over softly sleeping rooftops

Inside my box of magic I will place
Blush pink baby shoes filled with the empty dream of feet dancing to music they will never hear
The softening ache of summers sinking as she soaks

in soap sud skies

Blown bubble gum clouds popping in the pursed
lips of a sugared candy floss sky
A dress woven with words and ribboned with
rhymes and

I will place inside my magic box
The delicate eggshell of my mother's face cupped
gently in my hands
Bottles of Christmas to soak myself in, tipsy tinsel
tickling my toes
Pleasantly plump pillows scented with pine and the
lilac whisper of lavender
The tangerine tang of sunlight tingling taste buds
on the tips of tongues that drink the sinking evening
sky dry
My grandmother's eyes, like pieces of shattered sky
The soothing sound of slippered feet on soft carpets,
suggesting cups of splashed sunlight shared
on bright mornings
sprinkled with sugared love
The tattered teddy I tell tales to,
whispered secrets beneath blankets of stars to button
eyes
that know no better
My magic box will be light as air
heavy as grief

Things I will leave out of my magic box:
You.

The Wild Inside

Angela Cheveau

The wild inside can't forget
She remembers every last thing
The wild inside watches as you leave her body like a burst bin bag
pain spilling out all over the carpet
Lying like a disjointed doll she gleams pale in the watery sunlight
The wild inside tucked away her pain behind her eyes, folded it inside her heart
She stuffed her voice down the back of her throat while you
battered through
the paper thin boundaries that held her together
You split her open, wide, an open wound
Stuck pins in the places you conquered
marking your territory
The wild inside won't be quiet though
Won't be tamed
I feel the fluttering of her wings unfolding
between the bars of my ribs,
a cage too flimsy to hold her inside
At night she searches the depths of the shadowy forest sniffing the air
for the scent of others like her
the whiff of the mother tongue
ear tilted to the wailing wind waiting…

She listens
Listens to their stories, finds solace in their songs.
Laps up their wise words, licks her weeping wounds.
They tend to her gently, dousing her fevered brow, dressing her in posies of herbs
By the flickering light of candles they whisper to her, softly spoken incantations
hushed mutterings muffled beneath the murmuring wind
She draws their strength around her shoulders
and she rises
She gathers her broken pieces up beneath the silent, spinning sky
begins to sew herself back together
Tattered, torn and ripped wide open she has nothing left to lose
She forges her armour from the strongest steel
doused in the fires of hell
Her sword is her pen
glinting bright in the silver moonlight as she sings her pain to the stars
She is rising
Rising from out of the darkness
with a howl that could split the sky
Alone on a mountainside
silhouetted against the moon
she has lightning in her eyes
The wild inside wants to be free and she is rising
Storms break inside her

She is feral, she is fierce, she is warrior
Tear streaked and dirt stained she rises from the forest floor dripping in strength
She is not coming for you
She has no need of you
She is formed from rock and moss, mist and mildewed leaf
She is made of sea glass and shifting light
She is the whisper of wildflowers
the ragged rage of the wind
the scintillate sting of ice
She speaks the language of the moon
Rising like the surge on a storm swept sea
her daisy chain mouth opens in powerful petalled protest at
unspeakable things seen by the light of the moon.
Cries that had stuck like nails in her throat break loose on the scream of the wind
She drinks the sky dry, drunk on stars
She is unstoppable
The wild inside knows who you are
The wild inside knows what you did
And she is free

Treadmill

Angela Cheveau

I will run you out of me
I will walk off the stubborn shadows
Of you that cling with skeletal fingers
To my aching bones
I will whip you off my skin
Plaster peeling from an open wound
I will walk
With glistening beads of sweat
Running in silent rivers down my back
I will leave you in the dust
I exhale you
Out of my pores
Seeping
Like poison
Your words no longer holding
Me back
from myself
I walk away from you
Towards the light
Towards my future
Stronger with every single step
I walk towards my own becoming
The girl I used to be
I walk towards her
My arms outstretched
And I hear her

Her voice carries on the wings
Of the bright spring air
I hear her
Her voice buried by pain
Choked by shadows
a long forgotten song
aching
to reach my once deaf ears
her silver syllables singing softly
of a life left to be lived
And so I walk
step after step
growing iron in my veins
my muscles regaining strength
Turning to steel
Forged in furious fires
Stitched together with tears
They hold me up
As each footstep makes its mark
Heavy
Determined
Strong
I reclaim my power
My story rewritten as I
Walk away
From darkness
Towards a future dripping
In light

Yellow

Angela Cheveau

Houses standing like toast
slices buttered with sunlight
oozing drops of gold

The sun a fried egg
sizzling while rashers of cloud
fry gently in gold

The world hits the sky
with a blunt spoon cracking it
open, spilling light

Buttercups hugging
scraps of sunlight to their chest
in a gold embrace.

Splashes of sunlight
jumping in puddles of gold
soaked in happiness

Sunlight tossing light
over her golden shoulder
in gilded showers

The love between a
sunflower and the sunlight

can never be matched

Rustic sunflowers
nod sleepily in a field
aching for autumn

Yellow butterfly
fluttering with wings of light
Sips droplets of gold

I finger the cracks
of life between the yellowed
pages of stories

Pressed petal pages
releasing the ache of the
heart for summer's light

Crawling towards death
on yellowing fingertips
summer's last gold breath

Trees dipped in sunlight
pressed against the blank pages
of the golden sky

Dry corn husks yellowed
by the tapering fingers
of gentle sunlight

Memories hidden
tucked like folded love letters
yellowing with time

Paper like parched grass
crinkling beneath my fingers
stained with history

Melodies aching
in my heart from forgotten
summer's dancing light

Escape to Narnia

Donna Smith

A hot summer's day
Reading my favourite book
Sat in the garden
I could hear children
I wasn't allowed to play
Imagination
Was where I would play
I can go back to that day
Life seemed happier
I had thought it was
Turning the page of the book
The book came to life
I became a child
I was Lucy, really her
Stood by a wardrobe
I opened the door
I stepped into the wardrobe
Aging wood surrounds
Dad's long suede brown coat
The one with the fake brown fur
I smell Dad's presence
Cigarettes and beer
It's cold, I put the coat on
I take a few steps
I'm in another place
It's a winter wonderland

The snow glistening
Snowdrops in my hair
The animals were talking
I tried to listen
The faun spoke the most
I saw a lamppost ahead
Yellow flame dancing
Enticing me there
It was like an old movie
The light guided me
I walked towards it
Snow crunching beneath my feet
Before I knew it
I reached the lamppost
Suddenly I heard Mum's voice
Mum calling my name
Is this real, this place
My mind transported me home
Sitting in the chair
Here again, this life
Clutching my favourite book
No-one else would know
It's my secret place
I can visit anytime
Escape to Narnia

Endings

Donna Smith

My life changed forever
Front door closed and he was gone
The unspoken death

Day to day restarts
Time passes, I die inside
No-one can save me

Endings bring despair
Try to believe, but what hope
Empty words of love

I exist for you
I long for you to be happy
Drink is all you need

My life changed again
Front door closed and she was gone
The unspoken death

Loneliness sets in
Unaware of loss of self
The unspoken death

Broken but breathing
Accept help, hope arises
The truth is spoken

Crossroads

Donna Smith

I reached a crossroads
Standing here, I feel so scared
Which path do I take?

All paths look the same
Familiar is a sign
Repeat the cycle

A safe option is it?
It has never worked before
Unknown could be safe

But which path is it?
It is not the path of fear
Or the path of doubt

A path without guilt
Manipulation dies here
Seeds of shame can't grow

Traps set for abuse
The path is free of eggshells
Yet I am still unsure

Guidance is needed
As I yearn for what I know

The wrong path repeats

A light radiates
The path of hope lies ahead
First step towards peace

Freedom

Donna Smith

Born into a world
A world of love, so I thought
I didn't choose life

I started to grow
My mind and voice disappeared
Fear and love combined

I longed to belong
Living in a cage called home
It was all I knew

You made my life small
I believed you were my world
Suddenly you died

Left no instructions
Isolated and heartbroken
This loss, I am lost

You are an angel
In death abuse disappears
This must be freedom

Another love arrives
A familiar presence

Conditional love

I fulfil your needs
My needs are a mystery
Invisible me

I finally break
I choose to end this sentence
Without instructions

Uncertainty looms
My awakening begins
This must be freedom

Habits resurface
My friend denial appears
Confusion sets in

Memories haunt me
Acceptance, I am set free
The chain is broken

Can you hear my voice?
This is me and my story
Chapter one, Freedom

With Your...

Donna Smith

With your mysterious past that brought you here
With your night and day city life
With your empty pockets of hopes and dreams
With your spring in your step of a new life
With your summer smile
With your cheeks of autumn glow
With your frozen winter toes
With your loyal companion Jessie
With your eyes of longing to exist to passers by
With your repetitive words and battered memory
With your nose that smells food reminding you of hunger
With your over scratched beard of uncertainty
With your heart of love and promise
With your poorly fitting clothes worn by strangers before you
With your well-travelled shoes
With your yellow fingertips of the old smoke
With your collection of cigarette butts
With your empty paper cup
With your plastic bag suitcase holding the contents of your life
With your scent of streetwise aftershave
With your last crust you feed the pigeons you know so well
With your brightly lit shop entrance step for the night

With your plush mattress of cardboard
With your blanket of yesterday's news
With your trembling arms you wrap them snugly around Jessie
With your twinkling blue eyes, you stare at the night sky until you fall asleep
With your dreams of better days to come

The Lighthouse

Donna Smith

There you are, a tall figure in the distance
How old are you?
What have you seen?
Who have you guided with your light?
Surrounded by calm waters or crashing waves
You experience the same as I, times of calm and storm
You guide others with your light and are selfless
A resting and nesting place for all types of bird
How proud you stand there, tall and present, yet so alone
Watching the sunset and waiting patiently for darkness to express your light
Please shine your light to guide me on my boat of life

My Magic Box

Donna Smith

I will put in the box
The yellow of a golden daffodil
A chatty cat wearing a cravat
The smell of soil and a geranium leaf

I will put in the box
A picnic basket with a cake of courage
Sandwiches of serenity
Red lemonade of love

I will put in the box
A boat made of jelly
A crew of lost loved ones
A lolly ice stick plank to throw abuse overboard

I will put in the box
A map to life with a road called freedom
A door to close and not look back
A window to look forward

The box is made of my shed skin
Sown seeds of doubt that could never win
Its hinges are the fists of warriors

I will start with a blank canvas in my box
Picasso's paint brushes that breathe life and colour

The last jigsaw piece, called peace

One day you finally knew

Donna Smith

One day you finally knew
This life sentence could end
It wasn't me; it was you
Whom I thought I could depend

What did I do wrong?
Intimidating silence or peaceful night
Treaded eggshells on the road so long
Easier to agree, than put up a fight

Rose tinted glasses of denial tossed to the floor
Still believing he had a good heart
It was not easy to see him walk out the door
The very last time, but where would I start

Start a new life of not being afraid
But without a controller, what would I do
No-one to approve the plans I had made
No guilt cards played when he said I love you

Learning to forgive myself for what I didn't know
As this was the love I knew so well
A love that would crush me preventing me to grow
Is abuse really love, I never could tell

One day I finally knew
My journey could begin
This is me, not you
Who has the good heart that lies within

The Relationship

Donna Smith

Love, lies, last goodbyes
Power, possessions, no confessions
Cruel, critical, analytical
Anger, alienation, isolation
Ice cold, drama unfolds
Mood, manipulation, interrogation
Silence, stares, suffocation
Choking, confusion, illusion
Denial, distress, duress
Empty, fine, entwined
Blame, became no name
Guilt, gone, end game

Where is my voice?
Donna Smith

Abandoned anger, cliff-hanger
Fear, freeze, unease
Heart holts, revolt
Choking, closed cage, last page
Mute, numb, nowhere to run
Eliminated expression, regression
Speechless, sick, no chick flick
Denial, distress, duress
People please to appease
Uncomfortable, used, abused
No respect, reject
Guilt, grief, disbelief
Blank, breathing, still believing
Perpetrator, punishment pending
Sad ever ending

If I were to see you again...

Donna Smith

Raging, revenge, retaliation
Bravery battle begins
Surprise, stunned, shocked
Trigger, taser, tumble
Torment, torture, trembling, tick
Feeling frightened?
Skin slit severely
Still scared? Stoned skull seeping
Beautiful blood bath
Perpetrator penance
Valid victimisation
Destroyed, deserved death

Journey

Donna Smith

Fight for freedom
Feelings of fear set sail
Scared of the sea
Strength seeps silently through my veins
What wonder the waves will bring
Colossal crashes certain
Cease crying, comfort calls
Breathe, believe beauty beckons
Better life, love lies ahead
Uncertainty, unknown, unanswered questions
Quit or quest
Familiar or free spirit
Seek safety, stability
Closure on chaos, control, cruelty
Melted mountains of manipulation
Blank book, bated breath
Dust down, dare to desire, discovery

I learned from the mistakes my mother made

Evie Angel

My mother served better food on bigger plates for the men at the table
Chores were 'women's work' even though men were equally as able
To wash and dry the dishes.
But I was taught from an early age
That the Mr Men were more important than the Little Misses
And that the uncomfortable attention and sloppy drunken kisses
Were just harmless advances.
And with my ugly boyish figure disguised in punk angst
I should be flattered
And I would get battered
For 'telling tales' and truanting from school
And running away when it all got too cruel

From childhood to teen
With all that I had heard and seen
Behaviour patterns were forming
Until they became my routine
And 'put up and shut up'
Was my new way of being.
Because I got given mixed messages

That love could mean hate
And it became 'rinse and repeat'
'Rinse and repeat'
But I could never wash the hurt away

Until all the anger and abuse made me an easy prey
To predatory men who would have their way.
Because nice girls don't argue
Or put up a fuss.
Be a quiet girl the subservient women said
Become one of us!
A Stepford wife
With no opinions or dreams
Oh! and don't forget to stifle your screams

Be a willing sacrifice to male privilege
And be grateful you were given the vote
Yet the Patriarchal Kings still reside on their thrones
As we try every diet to stay skin and bones.
Silencing our voices of rebellion and dissent
Because of generational patterns
passed on like a virus
Creating another chain of violent events.
As another woman falls victim to abuse and control
Losing herself as domestic abuse takes a hold
Because 'you made your bed now lie in it'
you are told
Destined to repeat the patterns of old

But I learned from the mistakes my mother made
And a deathbed apology prompted a change
To help me break free from the suffrage of times past
And I found the courage to find freedom at last.
Becoming the kind of mother mine would have liked
to have been
If she had learned the mistakes her mother
and her mother's mother had made
to lift the gender smokescreen
Breaking down the generational expected victimhood
Building a new future based on empowerment and
love

So I am thanking all the mothers and grandmothers
now passed
Who challenged inequality
and were suffragettes in their marriages
Passing on each little bit of rebellion
down through my DNA
Enabling me to have the courage to demand equal
rights
And have my voice heard today

She was a mix of magic and mental health

Evie Angel

She was a mix of magic and mental health,
wanting to be Siouxsie Sioux, Nico and Patti Smith cool
with psychobilly hair,
wearing handmade dresses made from 1950s curtains
from charity shops in Liverpool
Not even trying
to fit her shiny star-shaped self into the square boxes
others wanted to put her in.
She was her own kind of ugly/beautiful,
held together by punk music and Paganism.
She shone far too brightly for some

Was it the hurt in her eyes
or the wide-open heart worn outward
on her baggy cardigan sleeve,
that he saw first?
Because you didn't have to dig too deeply to reveal her pain
It showed just above the surface of her self-harmed skin and eating disordered bones
Her wide smile and wild child eyes
couldn't hide what she felt inside
Her easy prey victim light shone bright
'Damaged goods' written in big neon letters above

her head for all to see
She became a sanctuary
for those undeserving of her fairy-tale

Already bloodied and bruised by life
she lost herself in the confusion of love, lust and loyalty
Trapped in a cage made of fear and self-loathing
her broken home heart still un-mended
And it felt to her
that it never would be
Her free spirit was soon caught in a stranglehold
she became less than whole
Barely surviving the abuse imposed
in a one-way street marriage
Abused and controlled

Her wounded soul
called upon every ounce
of her resilience and strength
to save her from ending this 'love and hate' life
With a head full of despair
and a handful of pills
The maiden, mother, crone energies
inside her rose
Reigniting the flame of her being
- Nearly extinguished
Hope restored
she escaped his storm

Switching on her goddess light
with a vow made under a moonlit sky
to never dim her shine
for anyone else ever again

The lost little girl grew into the wild hearted woman
she was always meant to be
A survivor
set free
Her altar destroyed
she found another altar to worship
...Herself
Performing a ritual under a new moon
with crystals fully charged
Chanting up to the Universe
    To take back her power
    To take back her life
    To take back control
    To take back her light
    To save her shattered spirit
    To heal her body and mind
Because as much as he wanted to...
He could never kill her magic.

My Freedom List

Evie Angel

Freedom is a safe house
With an open door
With a solid foundation
And no restrictive walls
It is a window
With no curtains drawn
An unhindered view
Of clear blue skies
And green forests
Yet to be explored
It is a book
With pages left blank
For chapters
Unwritten
It is a clock
With no curfew hour
And no frantic check-in phone calls
Nights out enjoyed
Without consequence
It is a body unbruised
And a mind at peace
A spirit reawakened
A soul undestroyed
It is magic unshackled
A self that is believed
With confidence overflowing

And self-worth immeasurable

It is a life lived fully
Without fear
With truth un-hushed
A survivor voice raised
Truth un-silenced
A whisper now a roar
It is a space
Uncluttered by control
Filled with courage
A half-life now made whole
It is a bed unmade
A pillow unstained by tears
Every second, minute, hour, day, month and year
Experienced without fear
It is a home filled with love
And laughter
Untainted by abuse
Undone from toxic ties
A truth set free
Destroying the lies
It is a future brightened
A scented candle lit
Protective crystals
Recharged by the full moon
It is music
- My mind medicine
It is myself an altar

- rebuilt from broken
A survivor ritual
Manifested
It is rooted in the earth
Re-baptised with fire
Cleansed with water
Energy rebirthed in cleaner air
It is nature my church
A free spirit
Revealed
And what was lost
Re-found.
Recalled to the wild
Embracing my inner child
Forgiving my maiden years
Gathering together all the crone wisdom earned
It is a breath un squeezed
A calmness present in every moment
A new coming of age
With a promise fulfilled
To set the caged bird free
To fly with wings
Un-clipped
Throwing out the nested toxicity
It is breathing in freedoms air
Into lungs hungry for a non-choking breath
It is a heart swelling with unconditional love
Discovered in my own treasure chest
It is dreams and desires

Unchained and floating high above me
It is hope given wings
To fly toward a new beginning.
It is unselfish self-care and self-love
No permission required
Under no containment or constraint
Free to be me
Totally
Unapologetically
It is a new path made
A solid footed foundation
Built upon the ashes of yesterday
A Phoenix lit from within
Reborn from the ruins of me
A Celtic Goddess spirit guiding every step
Of my new way of being
The ruling king
Dethroned
As I become the Queen
Of my own happy ever after
It is the caterpillar years
Cocooned safely
Wings drying in sunshine
Without the shadow of despair
My butterfly chapter now begun
- Freedom is me

The Journey

Evie Angel

I dreamt of wings and freedom
The scent of bravery filled the air
Courage rose in tired bones
Eggshell steps crunched beneath my feet
Broken glass turns to grass
Cross words led to a crossroads
And my survivor journey begins.
'Which way shall be my witch way?'
As I call upon the Spirit of the North
Tis the season of Winter
And the element of Earth
'Will I survive yet another winter's bitter hardship
if I stay?
Or shall I choose a new direction and find a safer
way?'
I call upon the Spirit of the East
And breathe in the air of freedom
Summoning Spring
Symbolising renewal and transformation
'Will this be my much promised new beginning?
Or shall I venture South?'
As I call upon the Spirit of Summer
With fire blazing a new trial before me
"What if I choose to go West?"
As I call upon the Spirit of Autumn
The element of water

Turning like a wild river
Embracing the ebb and flow
Reconnecting with all that is above me
and below
Treading lightly on weary feet
As I walk the tightrope between fear and hope
Balancing between 'Should I stay or should I go?
As I quicken my pace to a hunted fox run
Entrusting every day
to the strength I didn't know I held within me
Until now.
Escaping my jailor turned hunter
As my caged bird
finally takes flight
Seeking refuge on secure branches
Searching for a safer place
To call home

If I were to meet my younger self

Evie Angel

If I were to meet my younger self
I would hug her tight
I would become a safe refuge for her
In a time of great unfolding
The origami of me gently constructed
with clear instructions.
My rites of passage known and unknown
Told in bold and brave stories
No fairy tales spoken
As we sit together
In midnights darkness
The cloth of my being
Draped in a beautiful tapestry
Stitched mindfully into a coat of courage
Wrapped protectively around us both
The landscape of my life
An illustrated map of mountainous peaks and mine shaft troughs
Rocky roads warned about
Wild meadow memories bringing light to my dark journey
My maiden self
Face to face with the crone
A survivor of so many things
Looking back with joyful sadness
Alive despite her battles won and lost

Her resilience shining like a lighthouse
Perched high above life's stormy swirl
A beacon of hope whispering softly
"There is no giving up in this girl!"
The blanket of survival
Wrapped like wings of freedom
Around the lost little girl I was
Courageously ready to live the life given
No matter what
Trusting the proud and primitive ancestral wisdom
Held deep within her DNA
Comforted
Cared for
Cherished
Lifted
And Loved
Living life her way

Undo

Evie Angel

Undo the hurt, the darkness, the negative labels
Undo the bruises, the kicks, the heartache
Undo the years of tears, the FEAR
Undo the constant struggle to stay sane
Undo the 'fight or flight' automatic response
Undo the love versus loyalty dilemma
Undo the silence – speak up, know your truth
And don't feel the need to hide your story anymore
Undo the damage, see the beauty in your brokenness and heal
Undo the sadness held as a constant and let in the happiness owed
Undo the love that harmed and find the love that heals
Beginning with self-love
Undo…
Undo…
Undo and be you

Memories

Irene Stuart

Memories shift like grains of sand as
definites become maybes
as what was colour manifests into a
dreary grey

That little girl did she ever exist
the little girl with toys reaching to the ceiling

I observe from afar as she plays alone
in the yard surrounded by high walls
I contemplate, is she lonely
does she crave the company of other children

But she is not alone, retreating into her head,
she is playing with Bally, her imaginary friend
Bally, her constant companion, her playmate
her confidant her childscape

Who is this Bally, the friend she infers is a boy
what does he look like, is he happy, is he sad
does he have parents, is he also three years of
age

Bally's dead, she announces, never
to speak of him again

What does this little girl know of death, so many
questions as she continues to play alone
in the back yard surrounded by high walls

Aged five she is surrounded by children
she is uncomfortable, she is defenceless
shy, reserved, she is alone, she is vulnerable

She cries, I feel her pain but cannot help
I am merely an observer from afar

That little girl, the mini me survived
this elderly me survives, so many
unanswered questions

Memories shift like grains of sand

My Magic Box

Irene Stuart

My box is made of ice with slivers of coldness
no sun will ever melt. Ice which will never turn
to water. A box to hold close to my cold, cold
heart

My senses rail against placing objects or
thoughts into this container but it calls to me
I am drawn to its shape, its mystery, its very
existence. I fear to ignore its presence will
present untold consequences

Pulse racing, I lift the lid fearful of what it may
hold. Water, all I see is water, its depth
immeasurable. The blueness hurts my eyes. It
beckons me as a siren to the hapless sailor
daring me to partake in this great expanse of
Adams Ale. The lid closes with an
uncompromising thud. I fall to the floor
I cry for my mother

I am hot, sweaty. I picture the water entwining
my body, enveloping me in its coolness
Resistance is futile. I step inside. I am frightened
I cannot swim. Sinking deeper and deeper, I
am drowning. I wanted this, I prayed for this
sought it, requested peace but now, now

I am swimming. I can swim. I have a tail. I am
a mermaid. I have abandoned the cruelties of life
I am delirious with happiness, my cup runneth
over

Embraced as their friend by a pod of dolphins
we laugh as I fail to leap as high as they. I am
exhilarated. I am free. Free as the fishes who
swim around me. I say farewell to my amigos
who salute as they continue on their journey

My journey has just begun.

Floating, mind a blank, just me, the sea, and
my fishy pals, bliss. Hop aboard says Mr Whale
We move through the waves at speed but I hold
no fear, he is my protector

Deposited on golden sands, I drink from a
deliciously sweet coconut. I declare to the
listening palm trees it is the best I've ever
tasted. Without inhibition I dance as if the
world is watching. My new found friends
sway in agreement as they dance to my tune

Refreshed, I step once more into the sea, fear
and trepidation conquered. "Take me home," I
demand of the crashing waves. Take me home
for that is where I long to be, it is where I belong

Cradled as a babe in arms, I drift on this ocean of
peace, closing my eyes as the cruel sea, usually
so uncompromising, fearless and deadly, wraps me
in its tender grip as a lover to the loved
A shaft of sunlight bounces off the box at my side

I extend my hand, the box is warm to the touch
My heart is no longer ice cold, it is pumping with
warm, red, blood

I lift the lid, the box is empty, empty apart from the
memory of the sea unbreaking my cold, cold heart

She Finally Knew

Irene Stuart

It hit her like a ton of bricks the honeymoon was over
the carefully choreographed persona gone forever
veil lifted as the scales from her eyes, a pantomime
prince in reverse
a stranger in her bed

Now her tormentor, her jailer, her isolator, the keeper
of the keys, the curtailer of her energy. The vibrant
fun, passionate, opinionated girl gobbled up by the
ogre

She an onion, peeled layers of skin languishing in
the kitchen
bin, a bruised apple fading in the fruit bowl

He controls her, manipulates her, pulls her strings
Powerless, her cries unheard, no escape, no way
out

Strapped in this roller coaster, this helter skelter, her
life a car crash, an accident waiting to happen. Scars
visible and invisible, pain etched in every pore, every
line, no laughter lines has she

She recoils at her reflection, who is this interloper
this tear stained mouse, this rabbit in the headlights?

She weeps
How she despises this chicken-livered imposter

He strikes a blow
It hits her like a ton of bricks, there strong and proud
emerging triumphant from beneath his
toxic love is the girl she once knew a secret smile
on her lips
No more lies, deceit, or pain. She walks away head
held high
The puppet master is vanquished

Snow White And Her Seven Lovers

Irene Stuart

The door slammed behind the cheating bastard
Thank Christ for that, thought Snow White, world here I come, let the adventure
begin
First was Mike, handsome, unimaginative, goodbye
Soldier Lee, young, fit, chemistry, loved to love. She cheated with Simon
Simon, driving instructor, cute, loving, but
Karl, her head swirled, her tummy did somersaults
Both fell hard. Sixteen year age
gap too much
Roberto, the proverbial Italian Stallion. OMG, the tales, but a lady never tells
Albert, Kenyan doctor. Statuesque, cool, aloof, mysterious, wore no socks with his
expensive loafers
Jack, teacher, roguish with a cheeky smile, promises unfulfilled
Karl, Age is just a number. I love you, you love me, who cares what the world thinks
And so they lived happily ever after

The Colour Purple

Irene Stuart

She waits, fear, clock ticks
captive, invisible chains
heart pounds, stomach churns

Key in door, clock ticks
anticipation, he appears
smiling assassin

Purple dress, clock ticks
lasciviously licking lips
indicates she twirl

She shivers, clock ticks
terror, trepidation
control, power, man

He paws, grunts, clock ticks
takes herself outside herself
where unicorns dwell

Lust sated, clock ticks
stained dress, expectation
menacing, fists clenched

Punch, slap, stars, clock ticks
hands around neck, cannot breathe

voice unheard, blackness

Battered, dazed, clock ticks
purple dress, purple bruises
lays in silent pain

Child cries out, clock ticks
soothes, holds tight, kisses gently
body hurts, heart breaks

Lies to friends, clock ticks
purple bruises, door ajar
knowing glances, shame

Packs her case, clock ticks
must leave quickly, holds child close
escape, freedom, life

The Yellow Balloon

Irene Stuart

The wind tugged the string from her clenched fist and the big yellow balloon went drifting towards the sky. Her daddy looked ridiculous as he jumped up and down trying to reach it
Though young, she instinctively knew he was behaving silly to make her laugh, to ease the pain
They watched in silence as the balloon rose higher and higher reaching ever closer to the clouds
She knew a piece of her was clinging on for dear life to that length of string, an intangible part of her being had been ripped from her small frame

Within seconds the balloon had disappeared from view. Daddy bent towards her, pulling the fur collar of her pillar box red coat tighter around her neck
He held out his hand. She took it willingly. Large and warm it enveloped her cold fingers. She felt safe

Do you think Mummy will catch the balloon and keep it for me, she ventured
For sure, he replied, his words catching in his throat

We must remember to bring your hat and gloves tomorrow

Torture Of The Heart

Irene Stuart

You spin around and around
Like a hamster on a wheel
Leave him they say
They don't know how you feel

You still love him
You can't let go
You sink further and further
You can't say no

Where will you go
What will you do
He's told you over and over
Nobody else will want you

With compliments and flowers
Your heart he did win
A wolf in sheep's clothing
He lured you in

Things soon changed
His power grew
As yours diminished
Your confidence too

Criticism, put downs

Controls the purse strings
You became his possession
As he clipped your wings

You believe all he says
Everything is down to you
You're the reason he does things
You agree that's true

You are ugly, you are fat
He pokes fun of your looks
Isolates you from your friends
Takes away your books

You are no longer you
You don't recognise yourself
He continues to berate you
If not for him you'd be on the shelf

He plays mind games
Yes means no
Where to turn
Where to go

The abuse is not physical
He says it's in your head
Mental abuse destroys the soul
You wish you were dead

It finally becomes clear
There is no doubt
For your own sanity
You must get out

You plan your escape
With military style
You take your time
Deep breaths all the while

You know it won't be easy
You have to take this chance
To once more sing in the sunshine
And in the rain to dance

You spread your wings
Confined no more
The beautiful butterfly
Emerges through the door

Released from your prison
Another captive free
You are now allowed
To be who you want to be

You call to others
Please make a stand
Although it will be difficult
Your future is in your hands

Take the power back
As a female you are strong
For your mental health
Please right this wrong

Kick him in the you know where
Let him feel the pain
No longer your manipulator
YOU WILL BE YOU AGAIN

Choice

Karen Fletcher

Should she return or should she wait?
He would be angry if she was late
Queue at the bar a mile long
Whatever choice it would be wrong
Rushing spilling the drinks an hour late
He was seething, oozing hate
His face a thundering avalanche of stones
Uneasiness grew into her bones
Through gritted teeth with an ice cold glare
'We're going,' he barked through a hard steel stare
His raging brain began accusing
She knew she was heading for a bruising
Nowhere to turn, nowhere to go
Fate had dealt the dreadful blow
He had decided the night was over
Led her away like a lamb to slaughter
Into the dark despairing night
Rapid through revolving doors
Head bowed down, eyes to the floor
She foolishly followed his furrowed frown
His stark, strides, just stepped on down
Burly bouncers looked their way
She hoped they'd ask if she was okay
They looked across and held their glance
She held her breath this was her chance
They looked away and kept on talking

She had no choice but to keep on walking
Sharp, hard stinging pain to her ear
She stared silently at him and flinched with fear
Spin cycle of thoughts bounced around her head
Don't follow, tell the men, run away instead
Strange city, miles from home
In the days before the mobile phone
She had no choice but to follow
Her head throbbed, her body hollow
As he led her to loneliness, distant voices faded
Her mind was mangled, her body jaded
Her inner substance drained from head to toe
She knew she had nowhere to go
She opened her mouth, but it just spoke silence
She was empty, brow-beaten, soaked in violence
She had become the woman with no voice
At this moment she had no choice

One Day I Finally Knew

Karen Fletcher

The day that I finally knew
That I had to get away from you
Was not a single, one-off event
Regular toxicity, gradual descent
No physical violence from which I had to hide
There were not even that many tears I cried
In the beginning, you were charming
Put me on the back foot, that was dis-arming
Swept up with the speed missing early clues
But way down deep the gut just knew
Six weeks in, I heard the alarm bell ring
Antenna out aware of that ping
I gobbled up glimpses of the good
In the trees, I missed the wood
Gigantic gestures, feet under the table
You never delivered, were you even able?
I clamoured for crumbs of affection
Couldn't see over mountains of manipulation
Blinkered, I made excuses to justify
Ignored what looked me in the eye
Constant conflict you created
I thought it would pass and I just waited
Walking on eggshells, you would dampen the day
You wanted everything just your way
Acting as though you were entitled
For your needs to be met, that was vital

You sought admiration, adulation, attention
It was all about you, I got no mention
I stayed for the promise of what could be
Puzzled by your lack of empathy
You moved goalposts all the time
I was relegated, I towed the line
Dictating the dynamic, you blew cold and hot
Ambiguity, inconsistency is what I got
Tight, tenuous, tension you created
My confidence cracked, self-esteem deflated
I cannot believe that I chose
For my boundaries to be bulldozed
I normalised behaviour I knew was wrong
Our sell-by date had passed along
You lured me in and I settled for less
My own feelings a cluttered mess
Toxic turbulence I lived in limbo
Could not accept it was time to let go
When I felt low I let you back in
That cycle would again begin
Forever the optimistic fool
Thinking I could be the exception to the rule
Then the time came when I just knew
You could never change and I didn't need to change
for you

Remembering That Poem

Karen Fletcher

She tried to remember the words of a poem she had written `Now how did it go,' Julie said to herself. She thought hard, racking her brains through forty years, until eventually she recalled the first two lines I went upstairs and he was there, but he'd locked the bedroom door, searching through my personal stuff, going through my drawers…

That was all that she could remember of the poem. But the feelings, the atmosphere, the look on his face, that all came back, along with the memory of what had happened.

She had tried twisting the round, wobbly doorknob of her bedroom door and discovered that it was locked. The sound from her knuckles absorbed into the heavy wood as she hesitantly knocked. He did not answer, yet she knew he was in there. The house was solemnly silent, just the two of them. Her parents were at work and her younger sister was at school. When Marco did finally open the door, there were still no words, just that look, a cold stare with his dark deep-set eyes. He took a step back allowing her in, almost in an inviting way but also in a manic way, slow but quick, fixed but darting eyes, his body somehow relaxed yet somehow rigid. She tentatively walked in, scanning the room and wondering why some of her belongings were strewn on the floor and the double bed, which she shared with her sister. The wooden, white-glossed door built into the alcove of the chimney breast was half -open, her letters and postcards were colourfully cluttered across the 1970's flock-carpeted floor. Ripped open. Ornaments on the white glossed-over cast-iron fire-place were unevenly misplaced and fallen. Her photos were scattered, faces from all directions, locations and ages, stared up at her from the floor. The family photograph with her parents and sisters was pointing towards the window, looking away. Her clothes haphazardly hung out of half opened drawers.

He locked the door behind her as she stepped in. She was puzzled, alarmed, watchful, her instincts hyper-alert; she always had to be hyper-alert with him. Saying something the wrong way could lead to an uncomfortable situation, an argument or something worse. She was alert to what she looked at and for how long, after a painful experience of him saying, 'Were you looking at that fella?' and she replied, 'What fella?' genuinely not knowing what 'fella' he was referring to but then would come the accusatory comment, 'Do you fancy him?' She learnt to always be aware and alert to the fact not to *look* as though you are looking at someone. If there were males around, to avert her gaze, always look in an opposite direction, keep eyes down. But she would also get accused if a male was looking at her, as if that was her fault, that she was responsible for where people in a pub randomly gazed. That she had done something wrong. 'Is he looking at you?' She would say, 'of course not,' trying to diffuse any possible situation before he would get up and want to cause trouble. It was important not to give him the opportunity to find something where he would get the wrong idea, and she would then have to suffer the consequences.

Her mind flashed back 40 years. She was back in the bedroom, the situation unfolded.

On the bed curled in a ball for protection, like a hedgehog. She remembered thinking to herself `get up and smack him back,' but she just froze. Marco was 6-foot-tall and she was 5'2". The funny thing was that Julie could have put up a good fight. They used to have 'toy fights' all the time, as teenagers do. She was strong, sporty and feisty and sometimes despite her small stature she could 'get the better of him'. But here in her bedroom, curled up in a ball on her bed she was shocked and frozen into a vacant submission. This was not a 'toy fight'. Both 17 years old, her first love. She didn't know what to expect from love; but she didn't expect this.

She cannot recall how it ended or even how long it went on for. He walked downstairs in silence and Julie later followed, with puffy red, tear-stained eyes and matted hair. Shell-shocked and empty, she went through the motions, one foot in front of the other, silent, even the usual stair didn't creak. Like a clock-work doll without a soul, void of emotion. She didn't know what to say, how to act, who to tell, whether she should tell. He didn't apologise but she remembers him saying he would never do it again. He would always claim that he would never do it again.

Who Are You With?

Karen Fletcher

We heard there was reason for hope that day
So I went to buy the card to say
Get well soon, my sister
Newsagent pulls out wrong card, wrong place
A look of panic on his face
I said no problem we've had news, a good sign
I never thought it would not be fine
It was warm and cool in the late August haze
An envelope of strangeness dropped its glaze
Stopped in my tracks, sat on the wall
No explanation I could recall
The phone echoes loudly around our empty home
My uncle asks if I am alone?
I ask him why? Who are you with he says?
I ask him why and repeat that phrase
Why did I ask if he was lying?
As if someone would joke about your sister dying
Actions became robotic, no thoughts, no feelings
Lie on the couch stare at the ceiling
The dog came over and licked my face
Never before have I been in this place
I did not know how to act
You must close the curtains, I knew that fact

Red Flags Hung High, Red Flags Ignored

Karen Fletcher

Carefree at seventeen
Around the corner yet unseen
Physical, sexual, emotional violence
Yet remain, wide-eyed, tight-lipped in silence
For others you fly the red flag high
Your own blood-red flag ignored, but why?
It wraps you tight and binds you in
Yet outside still smile and grin
Hiding bruises, hiding truth
If Lynn knew, she would hit the roof
Speak loud at rallies against oppression
Why put up with your own repression?
You gave him chance, after chance after chance
You own feet bound, denying your own dance
Progress through life, still make wrong choice
In forty years you find your own true voice
You will through many of life's tests
Learn that loving yourself is best

They Looked Back Over Their Shoulder One Last Time

Karen Fletcher

They wandered along the dusty, bumpy, road to Chittagong, happily debated whether to get the over-crowded and often sweaty small bus or the less-sweaty, equally over-crowded train. Julie was not keen on the train, as during their last journey, lulled by its rocking into a semi-slumber, a man had placed his hairy hand just above her knee. She had slowly opened her eyes, freezing at the sight. Karina looked him in the eye with the, 'hard-knock' glare she could muster up, and in fairness, she had many stored up her in her 'facial expression' compartment. She stared at the man as if piercing through him with her stare, her neck stuck forward in pigeon-style, wearing a furrowed frown with her lips tightly pursed as she simultaneously picked up his sweaty, dirty finger-nailed hand. With a quick swoosh she flicked it down, letting out a teeth-sucking tut in the process. She then wiped both her hands together as if she had just picked up some donkey dung and was shaking of the excess germs. Karina was more the risk-taker of the two and ready for a fight or to 'front' someone, with good instinct for how far to push it; who was likely to back down or who would take the aggression further. It could have been instinct or a result of working in Liverpool's most notorious and roughest pub, where she had witnessed various 'kick-offs'.

Karina had experienced stand-offs with many a man. Even if it was a gang of teenagers, she would make her decision based on how someone looked; a confident stance meant that they were prepared to 'have a go', while a hesitant glance away with slightly nervous shoulders down told her they were ready to back down.

She would aweigh up her options of what to do next if they were to become more aggressive. Would she be prepared to hit them back? She would consider how many of them there were and the likelihood of them all `jumping' her. She was strong and fit, giving her a good chance one-to-one even though she was old enough to be their mother. If they pulled a knife out on her, weighing up who was in the vicinity, who would hear and help in that scenario?

In the end, she knew it could only ever be in self-defence, as she would lose her job as a social worker if she had a criminal record.

So, on the train to Kolkata, she took the chance to be aggressive with Mr Hairy Hands, assessing that there were too many people around for him to attack her.

Julie and Karina laughed about that man as they continued along the road to Chittagong. Their giggles drowning out the distant sounds of hundreds of beeping scooters and car horns. The lime-green fields lined the burnt brown stony road, vivid against the brilliant blue sky. They could taste the bronze dust, which clung to their damp skin mixed with the humidity and sun cream, gritty against their tanned faces. The smell of fresh lemon grass and baked raw sewage from a gully which ran alongside the field filled their nostrils. They came across a woman standing at the side of the road in a beautifully bright pink and yellow embroidered sari. Her posture was all wrong, hunching in her colourful clothes, as though cowering in against something. That was when they saw the man, his clenched fist raised above her shoulders, revealing the yellow sweat stains on his white linen shirt. She hid her face as Julie and Karina approached and he quickly lowered his arm.. Karina's stomach turned, her breath became shallow and her heartbeat loudly pulsating within her ribcage. Her body stiffened automatically as it took her back to her own experience in her younger days.

Julie whispered, 'Did he just hit her?'

Karina replied, 'I don't know, did you see him hit her?'

'No, but it didn't feel right.' Julie glanced around after if looking for someone to tell. but the long dusty road was empty. They discussed about how they didn't speak the language, wondered what they could do, who would they tell and what could they say? After all they didn't actually see anything actually happen. They looked back and seen the couple walking off in the opposite direction with the woman, head bowed about 8 feet behind the man. Julie and Karina stood still, looked at each other, 'Bastard,' Karina said. They looked back over their shoulder one last time, powerless.

Get Away

Karen Fletcher

To get away she
Waded through week-old red wine in broken flip flops
Had her spleen stamped on with studded steel shoes
Rolled through barbed wire razor fences raw
Had her body battered, bruised with broken beer bottles
Tiptoed through trees of treacle in tap-shoes
Felt the ferocious furnace fires on her face
Climbed craggy, cliffs coated in creosote
Tasted tasers on the tip of her tongue 'til it tore
Heard howls of hungry hounds hunting her
But staying away was harder
At first

What You Would Find In A Thrift Shop

Laura Lee Maines

I feel my heart racing
I can barely sit still
I am off to hunt treasure
Brought a big bag to fill
There's certainly something
That can come home with me
I can only imagine the things I might see
On the outside through a window
I see a mannequin in gear
In a suit made for snow
Only worn twice last year
And a bucket of shovels
Neon pink, yellow, and green
Meant for a beach far away
And little hands that aren't clean
A pair of black shiny shoes
With a scuff on the toe
Seen many floors in its day
Hand jives, Do-si-do
Stacked on a crate
That says coca cola
And tucked in the side is a
Brand new lint roller
Ding ding at the door
To announce it's been opened
And then shelves brimming to the right

Of little pumps to put soap in
And a selections of cups like in Indiana Jones
If you drink from the wrong one
you'll turn into bones
And every frame in a colour or size
To fit any thing you've got
Every spoon, every mug
Any pan, any pot
Then I see a display that's fit for a
Costume queen
Brooches and pins and a thousand shiny gold and
silver rings
My ring finger is a sausage
So imagine my surprise
When I slipped on one I liked
And it was perfectly my size
Hello you. I wiggle my finger
And then I move on
to the small little section
Devoted to lawns
And under the hand rake and discarded pots
Is yarn and needles and cloth tied in knots
I'm American, but I think you call them plasters
For cuts and what not
Here they sell half a box, just 50p for the lot
I suppose that's a bargain
But why only half
I can't ask the owner but it
Does make me laugh

Boxes and boxes of vinyl records
The themes to every war
School dances from before
When your dad came to the door. TURN. THAT. DOWN.
A song for every second of a life
A butter knife
A book about a crabs
And a scarf
And a metal contraption that helps you grab
I think the greatest find
Besides decorative fruit
Was still in its box
This adult sumo suit
Yes, I am wearing it now as I write
And I will wear it as I cook my supper tonight
I might even wear it to go to the shop
I can just imagine their face
When I waddle into the co-op

Unexpected

Laura Lee Maines

Only I was lost and lonely
Only I was free
To come and go, but on my own
no future did I see

Always in a tunnel
Always without light
Barely motivated every day
and every night

Maybe I'll adventure
Maybe I'll just see
Where my ticket wants to take me
and escape melancholy

Never had I ever flown. Never had I planned
to see you or to meet you
But now I understand

Hostage Situation

Laura Lee Maines

Love **is not** meant to be a hostage situation.
It should make you feel safe

You can't kidnap people with broken promises
You can't aim your anger at their temples
and demand that they do what you want

When you ask to love a woman with children
they come as a set

You don't get to say you'll send them away
because you want her all to yourself
They aren't complications
They aren't insignificant

Maybe you don't have the sense enough to care about
them
but she does
She would die for them

You don't get to tell her to choose between the ones
she had before you
or the one you made together

She'd never pick because they are her world
You told her to choose this or that

Stay with you or get the fuck out

Love should never make you pick your place
It should sit with you

You can hide inside yourself if you want
but it's not going to last forever
You need to give up because you are surrounded

Everyone will know you terrorized them
That you threatened them and felt no remorse

Love doesn't come from fear
It comes from patience and respect

You wanted something you didn't deserve
so you just tried to take it

They will all say you were such a nice guy

That you smiled and waved by your car
on the way to work every morning
It will be a shock to learn you aren't anything like
you pretended to be

Love should never negotiate with terrorists.
It should set you free

You'll have to come out with your hands up

I Need a Minute

Laura Lee Maines

People think I am so strong and so funny
When really I am barely holding myself together
They tell me not to talk so much
They tell me to learn to lie
I can only be who I am and I can only try

I think it's hard for me to understand the rules
When they always change
Because you either want the truth
Or you don't
And I think it's strange

How if I hand out who I am
And I bare it all
That instead of embracing me
It's used in my downfall

Like every little piece is stored in some gigantic book
And whipped out on a darkened day
Just for all to look
And expose my deepest secrets
Like panties on the line
For pointing and for laughing
As if mocking me is fine

No one sweeps up what they've broken

They don't stick around to see
The wasted and the wanton
The shadow that is me

They don't see the evidence
The life they left in tatters
Because when everything is said and done
Their truth is all that matters

And we wonder why the happiest people
Hang from strings
Why we stop seeing them on the street
It's because they can't bear to face the world
Or walk where eyes can meet

Because when someone suffocates
No one wants to know
It's hard to pretend that you're OK
When you feel like you should go

And I know you'll read this
And think my god is she OK?
I am just telling you what I'm thinking
Because today is my down day

I'm allowed to not be OK
I just need a minute

Returning

Maria Gornell

I look for him with kind eyes
that hold a wealth of emotion
with power enough to invoke
my devotion. That show me
the masculine force
of something greater
than all my false perceptions
But first
I look to myself with kind eyes
blurred through a haze of
shadow, that ache for a time
I was full - re splendid
pregnant with wonder
vitality and joy for life
I look to myself
first in awe

Unknown

Maria Gornell

They say it takes six weeks for a narcissist to realise
you're gone. It forgot to mention how long it takes
or the victim to stop waiting for an apology
a sign the person has a conscience
a flicker of hope this world is not so cruel
But the weeks have passed with only a memory
an evil grin staring back
last abusive words
fat stupid bitch whore
'It doesn't matter how it started
this is how it ends.'

Now there is space
traces of my lips on windows
fingers cold
aching
the early morning dew
a sunset that promises
new beginnings hung
uncertain on horizon.
I let a scab form over the wound
you left
sometimes I am tempted to pick it
how dark the colour of my blood runs?
the disappointment in my veins
Our story

dead weight.
Stayed too long
swallowed my mother's worth
my father's demons
you showed no mercy
and I
I fucked the soul
sucked the juice
you stole my words
I stole your notes
I fucked the nomad
into submission
and made him wait
for a ghost

'It doesn't matter how it started
this is how it ends…'

Me too

Maria Gornell

Somebody laughed behind my
resolve; in the kitchen
bottles clanked. A hamper of
plenty to numb her

In the parlour with the radio gram
they played John Lennon
I imagined a different world
but what is this idea, peace?

I tiptoe around. I am the baby
silenced in hushed whispers
choke on their screams
taste the liquor
and belch
bubbles in the air

I have a room
a box with a ballerina
my mother shows me
diamonds and gold
this is her way
to hug me

Lights out
I astral travel

eyond Huyton
the room spins
and shouts grow louder
I must not breathe

He saw me in my pale
blue nightie
floating; said I existed
waited for me
with some sinister kiss

the Bluebeard of dreams
till I danced in blood
then sacrificed my meat

Quiet woman, he said
then left

Blood and Fire

Maria Gornell

Red Rage lobotomy
Blue siren scream
Father stolen
Princess no more

A red princess chariot
Steel edged shoes
Luke Skywalker light sabre
Snapped
My mother's hysteria
A pocket of black salt

Muffled voices downstairs
Laid out slab
Cut from throat to gut

Loves prison
The dance of death

Love in a time of pandemic

Maria Gornell

How many suicides this month?
How much mental illness?
How many domestic violence incidents?
Did you turn up your TV when you heard the shrieks?
Did you clap while the bi polar across the street
barricaded herself between walls
co-dependent on the punch-drunk boxer
who uses her as a bag?
Do you hear the bottles filling the wheelie bins
smell the manufactured poison skunk
hear a cracked laugh
and more clapping?
How many will come out of this dead
and it won't be Corona that killed them
but the failure of care in a system
that bleeds disassociation?
Can you blame their tired bruised bodies
reaching for the only connection they know?
I am not superior in my self-made meditation
room that screams survival
as I breathe and chant my own wounds away
It could easily have been me

I travel

Maria Gornell

I travel
within the crevices
dark caves
of an innocent heart
past broken threads
blocked veins
black curdled blood
fight or flight senses
towards a gateway
some escape from
this purgatory
past demons, abusers
lovers and failings
I travel
brave heart
warrior princess
alert antennae
willingness to heal
Forty plus years
of carrying trauma.
I travel
deep within
I find her
sweet lonely child
beauty unravelling
loveless languishing

between worlds
abandoned
I travel back
to her courage
dancer of grace
smiling faceless
reunited with body
and soul.
Back through raging fires
torrential storms
ferocious winds
Deep rooted past skeleton
bones into crystallised earth
through tunnels screaming
to be unchained
Into calm waters
feet dangling
carefree,
laughter is the sound
mingled with waterfalls
nature and a heart beating
with love.
We travel back to peace

A poem for death

Maria Gornell

Some men will have you live a fantasy
a fairy-tale beheading of self
honey sweet words dripped
into the death of you

But I had my famine of words
I've known years of alone
empty loveless beds
and my disconnected body

You cannot tame my dance
or make me believe in
a love without discernment

I'll live only with the reality
of my skeleton woman
dragged crying pathetic
from the depths

and a man who does not run
from the horror of my truth

Apart

Maria Gornell

Alone
but not lonely
I listen for the night
its blue peace surrounds me
the moon is void
all is calm
I write poems to please myself
my audience left long ago
everything has a sell by date now
if you remove yourself from the public
hunger of blood
you become oblivious
you hardly exist
and yet you are free

Mediocrity is worshipped
while the wise live on
in their quiet lives
in their gardens
clutching their books
mirrors reflect only
their acceptance.
I haven't developed this inner strength
enough to see
past all gates
in the strong winds of my desires

in my waters breaking
that I am more silent
than before
and yet I sing
I sing my own flesh
into being
I am apart of nothing
and yet I belong
everywhere

Anima Mundi

Maria Gornell

Falling like yellow and golds
all the colours of my longing
to be less invisible
for the light to catch
the dullness of my eyes
I am in this poem
simultaneously
breathing and drowning
I can no longer hide
behind my words

All these dangerous yearnings
so natural like the death
between my legs
the sacrifice of my blood
and he that anima loiters
a volatile energy he calls
it love and I laugh
in some absurdity

Outside in cold air
fatigued; bone tired
age creeps the wasted
years of being sold
a fantasy

Frankie Ocean's song pink + white
soothes the vacant blue
coat - empty cups
and yearning connection
as the insanity of the world
turns

Bed of shame

Maria Gornell

A silent scream
the same uncontrollable sobs
a purple bruise inside
Patriarchy blinded - misguided
they ask us, with urgency, why
we stayed
with urgency
the way my heart loved
even the shadows
as I abandoned myself
They stare in a pitiful pathetic way
how could they know this?
violent storm as child
we recognised
anger as love
If I could reassure his demons
and mine; I am saved
not drowning in this flesh
hiding my fully bloomed self
I give body and blood
lie apart like corpse
flinch from blows
swallow words
He is my monster father
with so many layers
I do not trust the soft

nor gentle
it's like the calm before
the storm
fight or flight; I'll die
she's crying inside
my heart closes into
a fist he cannot climb
inside

They say it's our fault
we lived

After Cacao and meditation

Maria Gornell

Heart resonance
An avalanche
Overwhelmed
attached umbilical cords
the birth of love
death of time
woman as rock
soft at her core
withering then blossoming
as cycles before
daughter and mother
to abandonment scars
when did her value
become less?
more in strangers' eyes
womb that held life
arms that cradled hope
woman that loved too much
enough, enough
Heart medicine
strung resonance
crone wisdom
child flight
all the women before us
gather with fire
waters break

hearts bled
shining with tears
Tears a river
taking us somewhere better

The DAA

Shana Begum

Every time I looked at the door
it reminded me of that time
I resented him so much
I resented her also
What a weak woman
What a weak man
I pitied them both

I daydreamed I was adopted
Someone would come to rescue me one day
I knew I didn't belong there

That day we were all barricading the door
He tried to hack it down
My youngest sister stared out of the window
Pretending it wasn't happening
My eldest sister looked after my youngest brother
Holding him tight
My eldest brother and sister number three
Holding the door tight
Hack
Hack
Hack
The daa was hacking through

I couldn't stop shouting at her

'Leave the fucking bastard.. you have us!'
Her battered face, her eyes looked through me
as though she couldn't hear my screams
Rage shot through me
I wanted to kill him
She sat, weak, barricading the door with us
In such a daze she was
Every push the door went. Back and forth. Back and forth
Hack
Hack
Hack
I couldn't believe how weak she was
Tolerating such abuse. We could take him on
There was six of us and one of him
She did nothing

That would never be me
I looked at her in disgust
I was so ashamed of calling her my mother

Hours later things settled. Still trapped in that room
He told us never to tolerate abuse from any man
Why did you beat her then? I thought
Hypocritical fat bastard. I wished he was dead

Fast forward, 2013, he got me in a headlock
The fear shot through me
I wet myself. I couldn't breathe

My eyes felt as though they were popping through
my sockets

Helplessness, hopelessness and fear is all I felt
My daughter, nine, rushed downstairs
She looked straight at me
I looked straight past her
Thinking of the unborn foetus within me
Deja-vu
Then it all stopped

'It's ok, baby... we were just play fighting.'
That look on her face. It wasn't hate and anger
Her face was concern and worry
Never would I judge my mother again

Trapped

Shana Begum

Trapped
Never felt freedom
Vulnerable Rebel
Fought for something I never had
Just knew I had to fight
After a near-death experience
I knew I had to run
Left everything behind
I never looked back
Shackles finally broken
Liberated at last
The free flow of freedom
The first taste of choice
Quenching that thirst
I now know souls are born to be free

Mickey Mouse's Hand

Shana Begum

Never was given a toy
Desiring love
No identity no hope

Jealousy of my brother
Hate for the other
Violence every day

Gender inequality
They were treated well
Mickey was the toy for him

School was my sanctuary
Feeling I matter
Observing all the others

Never had a voice back then
Bullies made her cry
My responsibility

Feeling fear and hopelessness
I need to help her
Tolerating my normal

The toy was broken garbage
Looking through the bin

I rip off the broken hands

Creativity alive
That is all I had
I made a scary weapon

The next day in the playground
I swung the hand high
I chased those bullies around

They cried and begged me to stop
Their eyes of despair
Never did they touch her twice

My reputation was born
Unpredictable
Fierce little warrior

In Gratitude

Tamala

To my daughters, my family and my friends, to those I have crossed paths with both in loving and learning.
To ears that have listened and held my grievous words in loving tenderness, never judging.
To those who have helped me in times of utter despair
To all that stand beside me strong and determined in this lifetime.
To the strangers I pass, endearing eyes that meet mine, gentle smiles shared... my life has been enhanced in the most profound and beautiful ways, because of you.
To the fighting, the warring, the heartache, the violent storms that crash within and around me.
To the days I have felt like I cannot continue to then realise I am indeed stronger than anyone envisaged.
To the ones that have arrived in my life to highlight what hurts in order to then heal.
To all the people who walk with me on this healing journey who are not allowing me to remain small, instead force boundless growth to burst from wounds that so strongly bind us.
To the realising that we are indeed unbreakable.
To the realising of who I am, who we are.
To the light that shines on formless beauty of our

un-storied selves.
To the realising that no matter what we endure,
we cannot be snuffed out, erased or forgotten.
To the emerging dawn of a new day ahead
To the everlasting beauty I am so grateful to experience.
To the sunkiss that warms my skin through seasons
To the birdsong that graces my ears,
singing the world into harmony.
To the opening wide of eyes and letting love spill from light
To the vast open skies filled with mystery.
To each sunrise and sunset
To the embracing of all the cycles.
To the remembrance and forgetting again.
To the forging our new pathways
To the collecting of darkened memories.
To the cycles and circles and all that is no more.
To the realisation that in our tenderness,
we can indeed walk without the holding of hands.
To breaking free from painful trauma,
to allow unconditional love and joy,
to flow into the cracks of suffering in silence.
To the beginning to love someone and needing nothing in return.
To immense growth that comes from hitting the rocks at the bottom of a well.
To the surrendering after being squeezed of the last drops of control.

To the giving of yourself to roaring flames,
hankering to burn restrictive walls to ashes.
To the emptiness in the darkest of nights,
filled with the beauty of the moon.
To those that embrace and envelop us,
when we feel so desolate, fragmented and abandoned.
To those who remind us of how deserving we are of tenderness and love.
To the earth that breathes beneath bare feet,
reminding us that we are home.
To wildflowers that dance in gentle breeze
To trees that extend for bluer skies capable of endless potential.
To this enriching life that reminds us that we are not broken,
but instead broken open.
To the discovering of love in every new day.
To the rekindling of passion for this life.
To the remembrance of who we are,
and all that we are capable of
To our fortitude, our courageousness
To the gift of letting go
To the laying down of arms
To reaching to meet outstretched palms.
To the gifts of our ability to stand centre of our hurricane,
and greet it with full presence.
To the realisation that we flourish not from doing but being.

To unclaimed love we are all blundering towards.
To the overwhelming fear in my constricted body, my knotted stomach, my pounding head and my shallow breath.
To crippling fear that steals joy from places
not yet aligned with my core self,
which comes so vividly to remind me relentlessly of all of the places
I need to open my eyes to really see.
To the overwhelming freedom that rushes through and over,
once we lay down all we so diligently carry
To the growth of wealth and endless opportunities that await us
only needing us to turn towards our own love.
To the portals of laughter, happiness and grace.
To the remembrance of whole hearted unconditional love
To letting love flow for myself,
to shine endless light on all of the forgotten parts of who I was
before I learnt to clench against it all
To the gravitational pull that loses its grip
whilst scraping and clawing in the opposite direction.
To the realisation and the unearthing of who we really are.
To the ups and downs, the waxing and waning
To the tears and laughter
To achievements cultivated and discoveries realised.

To our overpowering undeniable strength and resilience,
our valiance and fortitude, our constant right to flourish.
To our courageous beautiful pure selves filled with endless wonder.
To the life and circle dance with vulnerability.
To the force of strength in and around me that is continually holding me up.
To the feeling of being saturated in righteousness.
To our own acceptance for a life deserved.
To the lifting of faces towards the sun
To the opening of hearts to overflow with love.

Dark vs Light

Tamala

It's OK if there are times when you are unsure of your next move and feeling completely stuck.

It's OK to not have it all figured out.

It's OK to have to go right back to the beginning and start all over again.

The truth is that life is going to shake you up more than once.

It's going to have you second guessing everything you do.

It's going to take you to your deepest depths to prove that you can make it out, and become better than you were yesterday.

No one said life would be easy, and your job is not to make it appear so.

Everyone around you is just trying to keep their messiness together too.

We are all imperfect but that's incredibly beautiful and our experiences are our badge of resilience.

You're here to live a fulfilling life that isn't about pleasing others

You're here to work on yourself, to grow inwardly so that you emit profound promise.

It's not about failures, lost relationships, broken connections, it's about you always doing the absolute best in any given moment.

It's about being wholeheartedly honest with yourself... as anything other than is self-deprecation.

You must realise that you're deserving of the purest of love, and the first step to finding this love is to go inwardly.

You owe it to yourself to heal the disharmony in the fibres of your body. Embrace your vulnerability and frailty you so diligently tried to protect from the pain of discontent.

Listen to your sensitivities, and don't let those parts of you go dormant, do not close your beautiful heart to this world.

Do not be disheartened by the unpreventable closing off from the foremost part of your soul.

Learn to instead open by continuing to expose your nerves and heart to the air.

Do not hide these qualities away in the darkness, because that is the surest way to harden a beautiful soul that was intended to be as soft as silk.

Your sensitivities are your greatest gift, be with them without the notion of frailty or weakness, to stop you from becoming numb to your intended self.

If you're living in a way that is less than you're capable of, you will constantly be chasing a life that's not meant for you.

It's about being the best version of yourself, to stop running away from your own darkness to not avoid meeting your truth. It's your time to start turning mess into messages of love for yourself.

To really see the things that brought the most pain, the most struggle, the heartache.

In the moments that required more of our hearts and souls than we could've ever imagined, and in doing so realise that real love cannot cause this pain.

We no longer need to turn away from ourselves and avoid all that we do not yet understand.

Although fear feels foreign and insurmountable unseen and unknowable in that moment.

You must keep turning towards yourself, you must remember that all that you require, all that you seek from another, is deep in the valley of your chest.

Regain your composure.

Step out of the story you've been wrongfully taught and begin to rewrite your own chapters.

You need to be strong, it is not in softening that you will find freedom, do not defend yourself, but instead learn how to stand in your openness under fear, anger, trepidation, under all chaos, numbness, despair, and desperation.

Build in your strength by releasing the shackles placed on yourself to prove to someone else how much they've hurt you. they don't lose sleep at night watching your struggle.

They don't suffer from hearing of your pains.

So love yourself so much more and release which you so painfully held onto.

End your own suffering in the plight to prove to

people, who are not paying attention, how much suffering they have caused.

It's an endless cycle with no winner.

Love them. Forgive them. Not for them, but for you... so you don't have to live in a story of disappointment.

Sometimes the greatest lessons we learn from come forth from our greatest pain.

Then we open up to the realisation that our self-worth and our feelings are not ever dependent on another.

That our story is ours to write - we're not the actor in someone else's book.

This is indeed your life. Go and live to your fullest potential.

We don't often get a choice in being hurt. This is unfortunately part of the dance of this life. We do, however, get a choice in what we do with our hurt.

There are times when you'll struggle to find an explanation for the hell you visit and the painful realities you face. You'll scour the earth for others to blame, in your victimhood, your righteousness, your anger, but please remember that this will take a large amount of your power.

Do not be held hostage by your distress,
do not let pain steal your inner power.

Your unrealised strength is in how you choose to respond.

Continue to grow, strengthen your ability to truly feel and listen to the wisdom of internal courage.

Its OK to speak your truth without the tidiness.

Now is the time to call upon the wise woman inside of you

Draw a line in the sand.

It's OK to rest and rediscover the parts you lost along the way.

Honour this time and space to withdraw energy from source.

Take all the time you need.

Words will keep on living.

You will not be forgotten.

To my daughters

Tamala

I'm so sorry for the times I wasn't able to love myself enough
I'm sorry for the unleaded parts of me that in turn hurt you
It was never my lack of love for you
Only my lack of love then, for myself
I was lost and in need of my own tenderness
This was before my soul pulled me ever so gently into light and I started to really see the world in all its wonder, and began to do the work to soften the walls I built around me
So, if I may, I'd like to pass on what I've learnt to you, so that you understand this life better than I ever did

I hope you never question whether you're worthy
I hope you realise you don't have to say sorry
for taking up the space you so rightfully own
I hope you're strong enough to always speak up for yourself
and to not be afraid to ask for all you require
I hope you never spend restless nights wondering if you are enough
because you always have been and always will be enough
You are magnificent in all of your glory
You are enough for the right people

those who see you for who you really are

Try your utmost to not deny yourself of love
and embrace your beautiful sensitivities and compassion
because they are your innate power

You are wise and have immeasurable strength deep in your bones
You are brimming with knowledge, wisdom and love
It's paramount that you're able to love yourself without placing any conditions

Do not let shame drag you to self-sabotage, stopping you in your tracks
Love and compassion for yourself should always be your priority
Please remember to listen to your heart first and foremost

I want to remind you, you are the earth that sprouts new life, malleable not stone
You are petal-soft, warm, loving and so capable
You sense what is said before words are spoken
and you feel the aching of hearts beyond shouting
you are supremely sensitive and because of this you feel everything so deeply
the power of the sometimes subtle is your guide, it's a magical gift

give yourself permission to feel all, in loving awareness

Do not defend yourself but learn to stand in your own openness, under fear, anger, numbness, avoidance, distrust and sadness as it's within these places you'll discover
the power of your sensitive nature

When you sense sorrow, this is your call to grow, not abandon
try your best to never deny yourself love and affection
and always let yourself feel your own ache, to bring you home to your heart

You'll come to realise good people will champion you
but you deserve to know that some people aren't going to stick around for you
and that is OK
It isn't an indicator of your worth as a human being, but of theirs

It brings from darkness into light that their story and your story weren't meant to have the same set of pages
You'll find people who will see your light and realise that it beautifully matches theirs
You'll meet endearing people ready to embrace a blank canvas with you

Painting the most exuberant pictures
Let the right people admire and cherish you for the beauty and light you so gracefully emit

There will be those who come out of darkness to try to steal from your heart
be wary and stand strong if you don't want them to feature on your pages
They were never meant to have a chapter anyway.
You are enough for the right people
you are worthy of true love
and you are magnificent in all that you do

Unfortunately, your heart will break
But you have the power to put it back together so diligently
Don't fret, I know you are immense in power
and you will overcome adversity you encounter

Try not worry, worry is a burden you must free yourself from
it's the heaviest weight that severs you from grace
and removes you from the ever-shifting current of life, your breath and heartbeat are your way back to love and truth

Life's lessons will equip and instil fortitude as soil for you to flourish
Never put yourself second to anyone

Never doubt your splendour
Always laugh and embrace when the opportunity of being silly arises
Always take the positives from every situation
You'll find positivity sprinkled everywhere
your light illuminates from within
and shines through, intimidating those afraid of their own shadow
unable to handle the exposure
but rest assured like moths drawn to a flicker
the right people will always surround you
Pure light has no shadow

Always aspire to speak your truth and stand tall
Always keep your heart soft and full of love
As it conquers all darkness and pain
Remember, you are an astounding human being,
for you are absolutely everything this world needs
and I am privileged beyond all expression, to be your mum
You are loved immensely by those worthy of you
Thank you wholeheartedly for teaching me strength, resilience and love
and I appreciate that you opened my eyes to the beauty and wonder in this life

Afterword

Congratulations to all those who contributed to It's Not OK, for producing such high-quality writing and being generous enough to share their work with us. In 'normal' times, experiencing domestic abuse is an horrendous experience, in Lockdown, as the surge in reported cases demonstrates, the horror of being subjected to domestic abuse has been amplified. We have huge admiration for the bravery of the women who have contributed to this book, and offer them our thanks for taking part in the course and committing their experiences to the page.

Writing on the Wall is a dynamic Liverpool-based community organisation, which celebrates writing in all its forms. We hold an annual festival, run year-round projects, working with a broad and inclusive definition of writing that embraces literature, creative writing, journalism and nonfiction, poetry, song writing and storytelling. We work with local, national and international writers whose work provokes controversy and debate, engaging all of Liverpool's many diverse communities in order to promote and celebrate both individual and collective creativity.

Our creative writing projects support health, wellbeing and personal development, and combat racism and promote inclusion and diversity. If you have a story to tell and would like to take part in one of our writing projects, or perhaps work with us to develop a new initiative, please do get in touch. We'd love to hear from you.

Madeline Heneghan and Mike Morris, Co-Directors

info@writingonthewall.org.uk
www.writingonthewall.org.uk
0151 703 0020
@wowfest